贝贝熊系列丛书
The Berenstain Bears

AF807962

森林里的幽灵
and the GHOST OF THE FOREST

小熊童子军去野外
露营一整夜，会有
可怕的幽灵去拜访
他们的营地吗？

第一时间的启蒙书

贝贝熊系列丛书

The Berenstain Bears

森林里的幽灵

and the GHOST OF THE FOREST

(美) 斯坦·博丹　简·博丹　绘著

Stan & Jan Berenstain

史 钰　译

父母和孩子一起阅读

家长和子女共同成长

新疆青少年出版社

“当心被爸爸发现！”
小熊哥哥在小熊童子军们
踮着脚尖下楼时说。

“我们不需要爸爸。”
小熊妹妹说。

“至少这次不需要。”
弗雷德表兄赞同说。

“我知道你们要去幽灵森林露营一个晚上！”

“爸爸！真对不起，”小熊哥哥说，“可是这次旅行我们更想自己去。”

“正好我也不想去呢。和幽灵一起睡？我可不敢！”熊爸爸说。

“幽灵？”小熊们屏住了呼吸，害怕极了。
“各种各样的幽灵！每天夜里出来游荡！”

“还有它们的老大——森林幽灵之王！取消旅行吧，童子军们。我真觉得你们不该去。”

“别听他胡说八道！”无意中听到他们对话的熊妈妈说，“有幽灵？别再瞎说了！”

“爸爸只不过想吓唬吓唬你们。出发吧，童子军队员们！”熊妈妈微笑着鼓励孩子们。

小熊童子军向熊妈妈挥手告别时，熊爸爸鬼鬼祟祟地上了楼。

他爬上阁楼，来到一只放破布的箱子前。熊爸爸要干什么呢？

熊爸爸在一张床单上剪了三个洞，把自己打扮成一个露着熊掌的幽灵。

领队珍妮和小熊童子军在森林边会合。“爸爸没有来吗？”她说，“这很好！”

“爸爸吓唬我们说，这里晚上会有幽灵！”

“幽灵？胡说八道！听我说——世上根本没有这种东西！”领队珍妮说。

于是，小熊童子军开始修建营地了——他们支起帐篷，

给油灯填满油，

点燃篝火。

珍妮抽空去周围

勘察了一番。

她收集到一些树叶，又采集了一些种子。这时，她听到草丛里有声响。

有人在一边偷笑，一边自言自语——你猜他是谁——是熊爸爸！

“这个游戏一定很有趣！”熊爸爸边说边把被单蒙在头上。

“嗯，”珍妮踮着脚走开了，“这个游戏两个人玩才有意思！”

她用一些树枝和树叶当支架，动手做了……

一张脸！

小熊童子军们围在篝火旁讲故事，过了一会儿，他们就都铺床睡觉了。

就在他们迷迷糊糊刚要睡着的时候，忽然听见一阵“呜——呜——”的声音，他们一个个被吓得从头顶凉到了脚趾。

呜——呜——我是这

森林里的幽灵！

他们奔向珍妮的帐篷，但是她不在那儿。“我——我们该怎么办？”小熊妹妹哭着说。

这时，一个更可怕的幽灵出现了，把第一个幽灵吓了一大跳。

我才是这座
森林里的幽灵！

第二个幽灵是谁呢？当然是领队珍妮了。就在这时，他们看到了——第三个幽灵！

呜——呜——
呜——呜——

就在大家吓得哆嗦成一团时，小熊妹妹偷偷地睁开了一只眼。好奇怪呀！她看见扣了顶黄帽子的南瓜头、爸爸的红色睡衣和一件圆点花布裙，看起来就像是……妈妈的！

“太好玩啦！”这是——妈妈的声音。她从爸爸的睡衣里伸出头来。

“教训教训熊爸爸，这么好的机会可不能错过！”

“这算两次教训，”珍妮咧嘴一笑，“世上根本没有幽灵这种东西！从来没有！不过，虽然这一点我们很肯定，但害怕它们还是很有趣的！”

The Berenstain Bears and the GHOST OF THE FOREST

Off go the Bear Scouts to camp out all night. Will an unwelcome ghost visit their site?

1.“Look out for Papa,” said Brother Bear as the Bear Scouts tiptoed down the stair.

“We won’t need Pa,” Sister Bear said.

“Not this trip,” agreed Cousin Fred.

2. “I see you Scouts are on your way into Great Spooky Forest for an overnight stay!”

“Pa! I hope you’ll excuse us,” said Brother Bear. “But this is a trip we’d rather not share.”

“It’s also a trip *I’d* rather not share. Me sleep with spooks? Not on a dare!”

3. “Spooks?” gasped the Scouts, not a little afraid.

“Spooks of all kinds! A nightly parade!

4.“And boss of them all— the Ghost of the Wood! Call off the trip, Scouts. I really and truly think you should!”

“Nonsense!” said Mama, who overheard. “Spooks, indeed! Not another word!”

“Your papa’s just trying to give you a scare. So, be off with you, Scouts,” smiled wise Mama Bear.

5.As the Scouts waved good-bye to Mama Bear, Pa sneaked around and climbed the stair.

Then up to the attic to the old-rag box. What’s Papa up to, the sly old fox?

Sly Papa cut three holes in a sheet and turned himself into a ghost with bear feet.

6.Leader Jane met the Scouts at the edge of the wood.

“No Papa?” she asked. “That’s very good.”

“Papa gave us a bit of a fright. He said there are spooks and they come out at night!”

“Spooks? That’s nonsense! Now let me explain— THERE ARE NO SUCH THINGS!” said Scout Leader Jane.

7.So the Scouts went to work setting up camp— raising the tent, filling the lamp, building the fire, getting it lit.

Jane took time to explore a bit.

She collected some leaves. She studied some seeds. That’s when she heard a voice in the weeds.

Chuckling and talking to himself in there was—you guessed it—Papa Q. Bear!

8.“This trick will be fun,” Papa Bear said as he pulled the sheet over his head.

“Hmm,” said Jane as she tiptoed away. “This is a game that two can play!”

Then using twigs and leaves as a base, she started to make what looked like...A FACE!

9.The Scouts told stories in the firelight.

Then they all bedded down for the night.

They heard it just as they started to doze. It frightened those Scouts from their heads to their toes.

10.They ran to Jane’s tent. But Jane wasn’t there.

“W-what shall we do?” cried Sister Bear.

11.Then, a spookier spook came into sight, and gave the *first* ghost a terrible fright.

12.And who did Spook Two turn out to be? Leader Jane, of course.

That’s when they saw— SPOOK NUMBER THREE!

13.As the campers and Pa shivered and shook, Sis opened an eye and took a good look. She saw something strange: a yellow hat on a pumpkin head, Pa’s red pajamas and a polka-dot dress that looked exactly like... MAMA’S!

14. “Just having fun!” The voice—it was Mama’s.Then her head poked out of Papa’s pajamas.

“Teaching Papa a lesson like this was just too good a chance to miss!”

15. “It’s a double ghost lesson,” said Jane with a grin. “There are no such things! There never have been!

“But just as sure as night follows day— it’s fun to be scared of them anyway!”